All Is Reaeemed
In Truth & Light

C. Melita Webb

Cover design: RLSather
Cover art: Selfpubbookcovers.com
Chapter art: opensourceclipart.com
E-book conversion: createbook.org

ISBN-13: 978-1535329989
ISBN-10: 153532998X
Kindle ebook ASIN: B01I8RTZCK

Dedication and Acknowledgments

To my mother. Thank you for being the first one to love me. You have wiped my tears, calmed my fears, and still find ways to fix my world. You deserve the highest honor.

To my father. You continue to be my strongest protector. Your love and strength helps me to see life's possibilities. Thank you for always loving me.

To my children. You are my heart and my soul. A body cannot live without either one, nor could I live without either of you. You complete me, inspire me, and touch me like no one else ever could. My best is in each one of you.

To the love of my life and the man of my dreams. Your love, strength, support, and dedication are priceless.

To my sister and best friend. Your voice lifts me up each day, and your love walks with me in every step I take. With you, my feet will never touch the flame alone. You help me find peace and balance.

Continued

To my grandfather, William "Ike" Brown, who is 98 years young. You forever live in my heart and in my soul.

To my grandchildren, who give me new reasons to smile, laugh, sing and dance. You are my unforeseen blessings, and you bring me joy.

To my extended family, my lifelong friends, and my children by choice, circumstances and blessings. Thank you for sharing your lives with me.

To Jennifer K. Johnson, Ph.D., for convincing me that my words need to be shared and that a book was already written inside of me.

To Ruth B. Hill and Emogene Price, for editing my thoughts, my cares and my dreams.

Table of Contents

Introduction

I have a deep love for humanity, words and books. I have always dreamed of publishing. This book is my first chance to share my thoughts and inspirations with others.

My thoughts and words help me to support myself and my loved ones through life's journeys. I write to enlighten, encourage, comfort and inspire both myself and my readers, for I find that I am happiest and at my best when summoned to assist others. Often the very advice I share is the information I need to hear most, or a lesson I need to remember. My hope is that you will relate to my writings and enjoy the journey through this book.

My heart is always open and willing to help. Since I cannot always travel to help, I give what I can, which is usually a thought to help motivate and elevate someone to take their next step in life.

Continued

I believe that writing from the heart can be less intimidating than trying to give someone advice orally, and when writing is done clearly and precisely, people will take note of what I have to say. Writing is like music to my soul. Words allow me to walk without moving, to see with my eyes closed, and to breathe fresh air into my day.

I hope my words will reach you with the love and peace in which they were written to inspire.

Chapter 1
In The Beginning,
All We Had was His Love

You are a daily beacon to my soul.
You help me stand when I cannot find
my own feet.
Thank you, God, for all that I am.

Let It Go

I have made you free
I have called you from darkness
And saved you from the great abyss
Why must you keep looking back?
Stop holding on to
What I have called you to release
Stop trying to keep pain in your embrace
When I have set you free
Stop calling back into your life
Things of no benefit to you
Keep moving forward and seeking only Me
Do not abuse yourself lingering in your past
All was reedemed through light and truth
Open your eyes and truly see
What is meant for you
Take time to feel and enjoy
The new smile I put on your face

Do Not Look Back

Stop walking back into the lion's den
I have moved you, pushed you, shoved you
And turned you around
Still you seek to walk back in

Enough!

I have made you strong
Do not lose focus
When you lose focus, you lose strength
Know your worth
Stop returning stone for stone
Wipe off your feet and march on

I Am Here

Trust, my beloved
Know that I am always here
My child, I know what you need
Trust and believe
That you are already prepared
With all that you need
Walk out on faith
I will catch you if you fall
Keep seeking only Me
Remember, I am all you will ever need

Give It Up

Release and remove
Negativity from your midst
That is not how I designed you to live
Remove the self-doubt
Release all the hurt, anger and fear
Trust Me when I say
There is more in you than you believe
I am the beginning and the end
I am Alpha and Omega

I Complete You

There is a special place
Deep within you
That no man can touch
It is I who completes you
When you feel lonely, lean on Me
When you want to talk, speak to Me
When you miss touch, seek My word
When you release tears into the universe
I hold each one dear
There is no word you can speak or think
That I do not hear
Each day you will grow stronger,
Wiser and more complete
You have always been
All that I created you to be
You may be there
However, I am always here
I will always be all that you need

Chapter 2
The Strength of the Next Generation

Baby, you just need to remain standing tall,
strong and free. You just need to continue to
be you, and to just breathe.

Essay Of Thought

In our culture, the old and wise often speak of generational curses. I believe the social patterns we see repeating themselves are learned behaviors passed from one generation to the next. We are now living in an informed age. We have access to news, communication and knowledge no other generation before us was privileged to have. With this privilege comes responsibility.

We must do better, now that we know better. We must wash, wipe and strip away those things that have not improved our lives. We must look at our lives with fresh eyes, see what we need to know, seek the knowledge we need to have, and build better foundations for the next generation. We can remove hatred, anger and pain from our lives and raise healthier families.

Each of us has a responsibility to love, nurture and uplift those we are around. We need to learn how to spot what triggers our emotions. We need to ask ourselves, "Is something going on in our present situation that brings up memories of a difficult past?" Do not sit and be content to be unhappy, unwell, unloved or unfulfilled.

Continued

Choose to forgive the past, and to forgive yourself, for holding onto it. Choose to start today renewed, refreshed, and committed to being a better you. Choose to see the blessings all around you. Can you see, hear, touch, taste, and smell? Those I believe are our first blessings after our first breath. Those fives senses are often overlooked gifts. When we recognize our blessings, so much more of life can be enjoyed. We must learn to be happier for the simple things:

A smile from someone you love.
An invisible bird singing up above.
After all, every gift is given in love.

Child of Promise

You are the child of promise
You are the gift of life, light and love
For generations your birth was foretold
You are the one who teaches us to smile
You see opportunity and endless possibilities

Fear does not know your name
Peace is all that lives in your spirit
Love is what walks in your presence
Joy is the effect from your smile
Calmness is in your reflection
Tenderness is your only touch
Mildness is the tone of your voice
Self-control is who you are

For you, my child, are the child of promise

Gifted Soul

The one no one saw coming,
Though we all knew the world needed
You, my dear, are a rare gentle soul
Your presence causes smiles
Where there once were tears
Your life gives hope
To all who know of your existence
You are the blended compilation
Of strengths from past generations
You are the dreamer of life's perfection
You are a gift to our troubled nation
You are the one who never sees danger
The one who never meets a stranger
You wake each day and walk out on faith

My Reflections

How could you not know your importance?
How did you not see the love
I placed all around you?
We were meant to be, you and me
Your birth was part of both our destiny
I prayed you into existence
From the time I was a small child
You, nobody but you, would ever do for me
Before you were conceived,
God took special care
He placed you deep inside of me,
Such a tiny seed
I watched you grow, felt your first kick
Witnessed your twist and spins
You and I are forever intertwined
Each day as I reflect on you,
Your loving smile and your intellect,
I am thankful, hopeful, and full of pride
You see, God saw fit and placed us side-by-side
Still today I reach out my hand
I am always here, my child

Looking at You

I see beauty deeper
Than what is visible on your face
Looking at you
I see 10,000 dreams
I see all the stars, the moon and the sky
Looking into your eyes
I see the dreams of the next generation
As your mom I can see
When you truly need me
I know when to step back or step aside
You see, I know you feel our deep connection
You are the one the griots foretold
Would live to see and make changes in our nation
You are called to find
Your own powerful direction

Chapter 3
Woman to Woman

Accepting where we are in life so we can move forward

My love— figure out what you want out of life. Think about the steps you need to take to get there, and point yourself in that direction. You are talented, loving, and deserving of every good thing you want. Remember, life, like any road, has its own curves and turns. You will need patience, love, a clear intelligent mind and strong determination to see yourself through.

Choose Love

Refuse to live in pain or in hate
Because you loved blindly
You could not see
Because you loved so passionately
Your hurt is still very deep
Because you still care
You have not been able to let go
The pain in your soul
Is your heart wanting to be free
Only you can choose not to live in despair

Nurture your heart and satisfy your soul
Then new love can be welcomed in
See with new eyes, eyes that are wide open
Love with a new heart, one more mature
Let go, because the past mutual love
Is no longer there
The tears remaining in your eyes
Are only hiding your heart's beauty

Continued

Choosing to move on
Is choosing to be free
Choosing to love again
Will show you have learned the lesson
Use caution, use care
But choose not to live in despair
You my love need to choose self-love
And to move on

What is That I See?

A pretty young butterfly
Stretching its lovely wings
With beautiful colors, accents
And charms so rare
Keep flying and reaching higher
Keep those beautiful eyes wide open
Do you see what I see?
The world is there, your world is fresh and new
Take a chance on love in all that you do
Smile when you meet a kind stranger
Laugh a little bit, but do not play with danger
Dance to your own beat
And stay light on your feet
Pretty butterfly—
Remember to use those beautiful wings

Your Next Step

When it is time, rest awhile and relax awhile
Choose the flowers you wish to pollinate,
And choose with style
Only leave your essence with the King worthy
Of your sweet juice
Watch out for the lure of forbidden pretty
Yet dangerous fruits
Pretty butterfly, awakening in your youth
There is time to run and fly free
There is time to dream dreams, love loves
And keep hope alive
Do nothing that will dim your radiant light
Beware of those waiting
And watching deep in the shadows
Use your beauty, talents and gifts
For all that is good
Make every entrance and exit
Only in God's saving grace
Remember, only you can choose your fate

To the Pretty Girl

To the pretty girl who does not look like me
I am standing here wondering
What it is that you see
I have stood in your shoes, walked a few miles
Of your steps
So you see, we are a kindred set, you and me
I understand the tears in your eyes
I see the invisible thoughts
Churning in your head
I recognize that strong, deep longing pain
Of your distant stare
Should I take a chance, open my mouth
And my heart to share?

For you my heart has always been open
When I am with you, my heart feels renewed
You see, that is just how deeply I love you
It was great watching you as the young princess
Now watching as you turn into the new queen
To the pretty girl over there looking for answers
Trying to find where you and your heart belong
Wondering where in life you should fit in
No one can tell you how to walk or what to feel

Continued

As always, I am here
To lend moral support
And a loving helpful ear
Now you are becoming a young woman
The world is yours, reach out,
Take a tight strong hold
To the young woman thinking harder,
Trying harder
Yes, honey, that is you
Only you know what it is that you need to do
Take your time, truly feel what you are feeling
Let your mind and your heart heal
Watch your next step so you do not misstep
Pretty girl turning pretty woman
You will one day be in my shoes
Choose your best options
Live life and love all that you do

What If

What if the next man
Who is waiting to love you
Is the last man
You would ever want to love you?
What if he is a good upstanding man
Yet not six-foot-one to six-foot-three?
What could you be missing?
What if, when he touches you,
Your heart would melt?
What if, when he sees you,
All he sees is God's beauty?
What if his every waking moment
Is spent waiting to love you?
What if you learned of the meaning
Behind his forever smile?
What if all he ever wants to do is make
And keep you happy?
What if you let your guard down
And left your heart open?

Continued

What is the worst thing that could happen?
You will discover,
Under the color of skin,
Beyond the height,
All men are the same
Why block your own blessing?
Why be blinded when you still have vision?
Why deny that God sees forever beauty
In all of His varieties?
After all, He made you
Let Him choose a heart and a mate for you

Sister Girl, You Are a Gem

You are rare precious beauty,
Really one-of-a-kind
Stop letting your self-denial
Blow your own mind
You are the prize, the gift
And the promise
You are the strength and wisdom
That built our nation
Raise your love vibration

You may be challenged,
But you are still able
Able to love deep,
Hard and strong
Able to hold tight,
Love right,
And support the right man
Release the toxic thought
That you will forever be alone

Continued

Look inside yourself
And see you already
Have a happy home
Love yourself,
Protect yourself,
And respect yourself
Relax and let Mother Earth prepare you
Keep your eyes on the prize,
Which is you

Chapter 4
A Day in Love's Universe
Celebrating Love

Heal your heart and make an inward connection.
Cherish your mind and enjoy your self-time.

A Mother's Wedding Wish

May you forever live together
And grow old together
May your family blossom
And your love grow
Always let God's wisdom
Into your mind and hearts
Keep God first,
Your commitment to each other next
Always be open to your mate's opinion
Let other viewpoints stay outside
Always wipe your feet off outside your door

Do not put your plans before God's plan
When in doubt, seek Him out
Keep your memories foremost
And when times are hard, reflect
Just think about your present love connect
Let your love for each other
Guide you, in all you do
Let your combined love shine
For all the world to see
May both your tender hearts blend as one
May her cold feet warm your heart
May his snores become music to your ears
May you grow old together
May your love last forever

Fresh New Love

Bringing in love as fresh as the morning dew
That is just how special each kiss is
From me to you
I remember the day I first saw your face
I remember my heart beating, increasing its pace
Then I saw your first sweet smile
From that moment you took my breath away
Each day has new meanings
Since I first met you
Each taste of life is sweeter
And has more meaning with you

My heart has new strength
And it now knows no bounds
All this, since I first touched you
Each smile that comes across my face
Is a reflection of my life with you
I remember our first kiss
It was a feeling I will never forget
I remember our first date
And each day since
My heart has no space
For anyone but you

Elisse's Poem

You are my love and my life
Without you, there is no me
It was written in the stars
That our love was meant to be
If you were gone
A hole would forever be in my heart
For you are the best part of me

When I look deeply into your eyes
I am mesmerized by the precious love we share
The path to my heart starts at your feet
For without you, there is no me

With you by my side
I have lived a lifetime of blessings
Together we are stronger
Than we ever were apart
No one else matters, and I know
You will forever be in my heart

Remembering Why I Love You

When I wake each morning
My first thought is of you
I open my eyes, look over
And a smile is born on my face
Whether you are awake, asleep
Or laying there relaxing
Your presence brings me joy
Loving you is easy
And it is its own reward

From the first smile we shared
The first touch from your hand
The first kiss we enjoyed
My heart has belonged only to you

For the warmth you are to my soul
For the comfort you are to my heart
For the peace you bring to my mind
For the happiness we share daily

I thank you

50 Years of Loving

Looking at the two of you today
As you celebrate fifty years of love,
Peace and unity
Gives me pride and gives me joy
Seeing you loving each other in a strong marriage
Proves that true love can last a lifetime
Looking at you helps me believe
That my dreams can come true

Looking at the two of you
Is an inspiration to me
Witnessing your love grow deeper, stronger
And better each day
Seeing you share love,
Hugs and kisses along the way
Loving each other through winter, spring,
Summer and fall
Standing the test of time,
And your love stands tall
Seeing you share all you have and all you do
Shows me that dreams can come true
Yes, that is what I see
When I look at the two of you

Continued

Looking at the two of you,
Watching how you care for each other,
Our family and our friends
Seeing your love is the greatest life lesson of all
Having you as a role models
Is the best gift anyone can receive

Watching the two of you living in love
Watching you plant seeds of love
In all who enter your home
Seeing you share smiles, hobbies, jokes and tears
Makes me believe in love
And now I know some fairytales can come true
Seeing the love in your eyes
As you look at each other
Makes me believe your love will last
Another fifty years

You two are a reflection of all that is good
And what is possible
For your love is the greatest proof
Of God's loving kindness

Anniversary Poem

As our love renews and remains strong
Your daily kindness is proof of eternal joy
After many years, millions of smiles,
Arms full of love
A heart that remains warm and tender
Enough joy to last a lifetime
You, my love,
Still take my breath away

After living, loving and growing
Our world together
I thank you
For when I am with you
There is no doubt
Of God's direct blessings
Years of living, loving, sharing and caring
Is proof of what love is
For what is love?
Love is you!

Chapter 5: Saying Goodbye
Retaining precious memories, releasing emotions, and learning to let go.

Not a day has passed since you left
that you have not been in our hearts
and on our minds.

My First Thoughts

I am glad you have found eternal peace
I have no regrets
I have no true sorrow
You have shown me the way
The way to live, dream, love and challenge

The world...
What more can my soul ask from you?
What more can we demand of you?
Nothing
It would have been unfair
To ask you to stay
And keep you in despair

I guess you can see you taught me well
You taught me to accept who I am with pride
You also taught me to choose who I want to be
You inspired me to write
And find peace in my own mind
No longer do fear, hurt, pain or strife
Define who I am

Continued

I learned new choices could be made
I learned new songs could be sung
And new steps could be taken
Through your beautiful words, poems,
Memoirs and essays
I learn that a better life could be imagined
And a better life could be lived
I learned that only the past has been written
And that the future is mine to create
I chose to walk strong in my own steps
Because of you I chose to break free
From the pain that was once part of me
An education I received
Which can never be taken from me

Our Child of God

Our child of God has been called back home
God has reclaimed his broken body
And made him new
He took him home and wrapped him
In the finest of silks and satins
God knew there was a limit
To what man could do
He stepped in
And He whispered softly,
I am here now, my child, rest
Close your eyes,
Take your last breath,
Just be at rest

He blew a wind
To place calm on his shoulders
God waved his hand
And took all of his pain,
His tears and his fears
God touched his heart
And let him know that we would be fine

Continued

We will miss his warm smile,
His tender touch,
Oh so much
We will wipe away tears
For the many memories
We shared
Memories of laughter and the smiles
He left in each one of our hearts
We will still dream, dreams
Of his kindness
Yes, he will forever be missed

Remembering Those We Lost

I love you
And I think of you daily
I am glad we shared great memories
I remember all the things your living
And loving taught me:
Love unconditionally
Forgive those who wrong you
Always stand tall
And give our best efforts
Keep marching,
Even when our bodies
Are tired and weary
We are all glad that you are no longer in pain
We are happy to know
Tthat you now know true rest
You will always be deeply missed
Please be at peace,
And do not worry about us

Continued

You taught us the true meaning of love
And how to live our lives right
You helped everyone in need
And never missed a chance to smile
Your heart was always open
Your caring ways touched each of our lives
We are all the better for having known you
Your quick wit, knowledge and keen intellect
Will continue to encourage us
Through life's joys and in life's challenges
The lessons you have shown us
Will last a lifetime

Ode to a Fallen Soldier

I am proud of you
And the dignity you displayed
As you fought through life's battles
I will always miss your big heart
And your deep belly laughs
The lessons you have shown us
Will last a lifetime
Your words of wisdom
Will be passed down for generations
No one who ever met you
Could forget your kind eyes
Your loving smile
Or your warm embrace

We thank the Lord
For placing you into each
One of our hearts and lives
We find peace in knowing
Your spirit has returned to God

Learning of Your Passing

I heard the news
And did not want to believe my ears
In a flash I grew cold,
Felt alone and seemed lost
And the tears begin to fall from my eyes
My heart ached and began to race
At the thought that you were no longer here
As I struggle to regain my composure
I stopped to ponder the meaning
Of the loss of your loving heart
When I stood again,
A smile replaced my tears
As I remembered all the wonderful years
Of memories we shared
Your love, understanding, acceptance and grace
Gave me wings to soar
Our friendship is priceless
And our connection
Does not end with your death
Your memories provide me comfort to continue

Letting a Loved One Go

Not a day has passed
That you have not been in our hearts
And in our minds
You lived well and prepared us to carry on
It is now time for you to rest
We know you fought hard
And you always did your best

We know your suffering has ended
No more tears of pain
Will you be called to shed
Through your faith and through your works
Your need for a frail body has ended
For in the spirit world a body you do not need
With God it does not matter
How fast we can throw
How far we can run
Or how well we can speak

With God it does not matter
How well you dress
How much money you can make
Or the amount of worldly possessions
You have amassed
For nothing from this world
Can be taken with you
When you breathe your final breath

Continued

What matters is the life you lead
While you walked the earth
What matters is the love you shared,
The hugs you gave and the people you touched
What matters is the lives you have enhanced
And the lessons you taught

With God it does not matter
How sick we are when we walked his earth
It does not matter
How physically challenged we are
When we take our last breath

All that matters is that we helped those in need
That we cared for one another
That we learned the lessons in life
That mean the most

Lives Snatched by Violence

Looking into your eyes
I see the stories you never got to tell
The memories you never got to share
The beauty that only now the world knows

Looking into your eyes
I see the dreams you left undreamt
The children you never got to bear
The laughter you had yet to cause and share
The tears that will forever fall
As we remember

Looking at the simple beauty of your face
I see hope for our human race
I see the tears of your painful fate
I see the love you never got to make

Looking at the symmetry of your face
I see the strength
Only you knew you possessed
I see the beauty of your soul,
Your style and your grace
I see the strength of 400 years

Continued

I feel the pain that shocked our nation
But I can never hear
The last moments of your breath
Nor can I see the scenes
You saw when you left
I can only wonder at the fear
That filled your dear heart

Your memory has now become a movement
Monuments will be built
Understandings will be sought
None in this man's world will be found
You will forever be remembered

Lives Lost Too Young

Looking at the beauty of your youth
Remembering the smiles
That once crossed your face
Feeling the traces of life you left behind
Laughing at the silly things
You used to say and do
Holding onto the last hug we shared
Touching the last spot you kissed on my cheek
Missing your sweet hand on my shoulder
Sharing the stories you once told
Wishing upon every falling star
Searching forever inward and deep
Looking for that special place
Where our hearts meet
Waiting for my phone to ring
And my door to swing open
Hoping for one more moment with you
In the end, even that would
Really never be enough
The only true peace will come
When once again I will be with you

My Heart is Heavy

Words have no meaning
When a loved one is missing
There is just despair
I am praying for understanding
When I know none can be found
I am trying hard to control my emotions
By limiting my sound
I am thankful for all the prayers, blessings,
Well wishes, thoughtful gifts
And everyone's concern
There is just an awful feeling
Like a deep heartburn

I am thankful for the kind words of comfort
And for the pictures and memories we all share
I am thankful for my children,
My family and my friends,
All who care

At a time of such deep sorrow
There is no place of peace that you can see
There is no part of your body
That does not ache
There are no magic words to say
For a pain that will not go away

My Heart Is Heavy Continued

There is little joy you can think of
But honestly there is nothing anyone can do
By my faith and relying on God's strength
I know I will make it through

In time the ache dulls
Sadness will lessen
And new joys will be found

~In Closing~

A Thought to the Universe
I am here ready to listen
Send me more signs
And reasons to understand
So I can walk through my life
As a better woman
Peace to the universe
As you heard my inner thoughts,
My outer cries,
Prayerful moments and occasional sighs
Please keep blessing me
As I am your faithful daughter
And I am now listening intently

Peace

My Wish for Each of You
Peace is loving yourself just the way you are
Peace is being healthy
Peace is improving your quality of life each day
Peace is sharing smiles because you are alive
Peace is walking daily in God's word
Peace is no longer raising your voice in anger
Peace is enjoying the people around you
Like there is no tomorrow
Peace is removing the people around you
That harm you in any way
Peace is handling responsibilities like an adult
Peace is loving where I am,
Accepting that I may not know God's plan
Accepting that I may not always fully understand
Accepting that I must always listen

I wish for you peace and understanding
I wish for you no more hurtful tears
Only smiles and deep laughter of happiness
To fill every hallway, room and space you enter

— C. Melita Webb

We hope you enjoyed book one in our collection and we invite you to continue the inspirational journey. All of the books in our collection inspire, motivate and uplift readers.

Poetry From the Heart books
by C. Melita Webb

Book one in Poetry From the Heart Collection:
All is Redeemed in Truth and Light,
Kindle Edition, ASIN: B01I8RTZCK,
July 2016
ISBN-13: 978-1535329989
ISBN-10: 15353299X

Book two in Poetry From the Heart Collection:
The Light That is You
Kindle Edition, ASIN: B01M72UNGO,
October 2016
ISBN-13: 978-1537781358
ISBN-10: 1537781359

Book three in Poetry From the Heart Collection:
God Placed You Here
Kindle Edition, ASIN: B074RJK56H
August 2017
ISBN-13: 978-1539816591
ISBN-10: 1539816591

Please visit us at www.cmelitawebb.com

Made in the USA
San Bernardino, CA
04 March 2020